Would You Rather?

Made You Think!

EDITION

Would You Rather? Made You Think! EDITION

Answer Hilarious Questions
& Win the Game of Wits

BY LINDSEY DALY

Z KIDS • NEW YORK

Z Kids
An imprint of Zeitgeist™
A division of Penguin Random House LLC
1745 Broadway, New York, NY 10019
zeitgeistpublishing.com
penguinrandomhouse.com

ISBN: 9780593196793
Ebook ISBN: 9780593197011

Printed in the United States of America on acid-free paper

15th Printing

Cover and interior art © Shutterstock.com
Author photograph by Image Art Studio
Cover design by Stacy Wakefield Forte
Interior design by Katy Brown

The authorized representative in the EU for product safety and compliance is Penguin Random House Ireland, Morrison Chambers, 32 Nassau Street, Dublin D02 YH68, Ireland. https://eu-contact.penguin.ie

For my parents,

whose unwavering support gives me
the confidence to believe in myself;

for my students past and present,

who have made me a better person;

and for every kid

brave enough to think
outside the box.

Contents

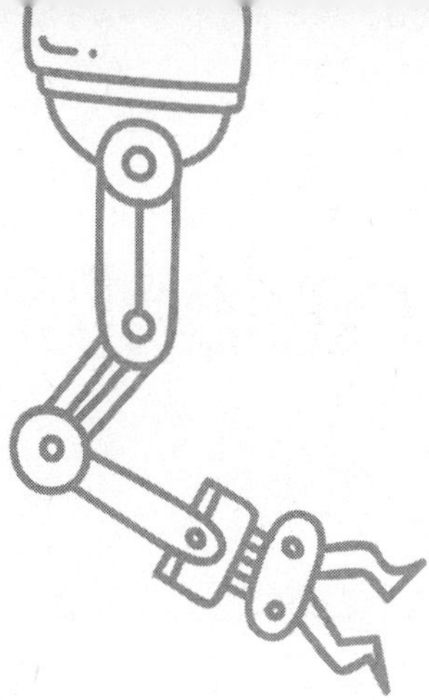

Introduction

The world is full of endless decisions and possibilities. Each and every day, we all make hundreds of little choices. What should I eat for breakfast? What will I wear today? Who will I sit with at lunch? How can I single-handedly overthrow all of the world's leaders and accomplish my dream of total global domination?

Okay, maybe not the last one, but you get the point. In order to successfully make decisions, we must be smart, take time to think things through, and use our creativity to find the best answer. But what makes someone "smart"? Maybe you ace every test after only a small amount of studying. Maybe you build amazing things without using any directions, or you create artistic masterpieces. Perhaps you use humor to entertain people, or you think on your feet and communicate well with others. Everybody is a certified smarty-pants in their own special way.

All it takes to navigate this ever-changing world is a mix of imagination, logic, and outside-the-box thinking.

In today's society, information is being thrown at us constantly. That's why it's important to sharpen those thinking skills and form your own unique opinions and ideas. The most wonderful discovery in life is that there is no "right" answer, and in many instances, it's not *what* you do but *how* you do it. Thinking critically and going on a journey to find *your* answer is where all of the fun happens. It's brave to question, explore, and think creatively. Plus, the best thing you could possibly do for another person is to challenge them to think! This game book provides you with 160 silly, fun, and wacky chances to do just that!

Are you up for the challenge? Grab a few of your friends or family members, and get ready to outthink them! So, how will you solve problems and make your choices? We're about to find out.

Rules of the Game

Get a group of friends or family members together for a game of wits and creativity.

The more the merrier!

* The game is played in 8 levels, with 20 questions in each level. As the levels increase, so does the complexity of the questions.
* Players rotate the responsibility of being the "judge" and reading the question aloud to the group.
* Players will then answer with an explanation and take turns sharing their answers.
* The judge of that round will choose the best answer—it could be the smartest, the funniest, or the most creative. Write the winner's name in the space provided below the question and assign

them 1 point. If only two people are playing, the judge (the player reading the question) assigns 1 to 5 points for the answer (5 being the best answer) and records it with the other player's name in the space provided below the question.

* When all players complete the level, tally up the points to determine the winner for that level.

* In the event of a tie at the end of a level, the two players who are tied will answer the "tiebreaker" question. All remaining players will vote on the best answer. If only two people are playing, whoever makes the other player laugh wins.

When players complete the book, the winner of the most levels is the champion!

LEVEL 1

Smart Starts

Would you rather
kiss a fish that's been living in a radioactive pond
or
roll down a hill while hugging a porcupine?

WINNER: POINTS:

Would you rather
have one best friend
or
five friends who don't know you really well?

WINNER: POINTS:

Would you rather
take a private tour of
a space shuttle
or
a submarine?

WINNER: POINTS:

Would you rather
get a summer job at
an alpaca farm
or
herding sheep?

WINNER: POINTS:

Would you rather

get stranded on an island

or

lost in the middle of the woods?

WINNER: POINTS:

Would you rather

ride through the forest
on a unicorn

or

spend a day hanging out
with Bigfoot?

WINNER: POINTS:

Would you rather
have cotton candy for hair
or
spaghetti?

WINNER: POINTS:

Would you rather
have a pet platypus
or
a pet aardvark?

WINNER: POINTS:

Would you rather
work as a
rodeo clown
or
as a lion tamer
at the circus?

WINNER: POINTS:

Would you rather
play a game one-on-one with
your favorite athlete
or
sing a duet with your
favorite singer?

WINNER: POINTS:

Would you rather

drink dirty dishwater from the sink

or

someone else's bathwater?

WINNER: POINTS:

Would you rather

discover an alien
in your backyard

or

a new animal species?

WINNER: POINTS:

Would you rather
have control over
when it rains
or
when it snows?

WINNER: POINTS:

Would you rather
get spit on by a llama
or
pooped on by a cow?

WINNER: POINTS:

Would you rather

spend a year walking on stilts every day

or

jumping from place to place on a pogo stick?

WINNER: POINTS:

Would you rather

use a stranger's toothbrush to brush your teeth

or

another person's used tissue to blow your nose?

WINNER: POINTS:

Would you rather
wake up one morning
as a mermaid
or
a centaur?

WINNER: POINTS:

Would you rather
spend a year living in an
igloo in the Arctic
or
living in a tree house
in the Amazon rain forest?

WINNER: POINTS:

Would you rather

have the ability to be invisible whenever you choose

or

the power to make other people disappear at your command?

WINNER: POINTS:

Would you rather

spend the rest of your life without television

or

video games?

WINNER: POINTS:

TIEBREAKER

Would you rather

be a passenger on the first commercial flight to Mars

or

a passenger on the first public bus tour of Area 51?

WINNER: POINTS:

WINNER: ______________________________

TOTAL POINTS: ______________________________

LEVEL 2

Playful Picks

Would you rather
throw up in front of
your whole class
or
fart in front of your teacher?

WINNER: POINTS:

Would you rather
have a robot that does
all of your chores
or
completes your
school projects?

WINNER: POINTS:

Would you rather
explore the inside of
an ancient pyramid
or
the inside of a cave that contains
prehistoric paintings?

WINNER: POINTS:

Would you rather
lose your sense of smell
or
taste?

WINNER: POINTS:

Would you rather
have a pet sloth
or
a pet koala?

WINNER: POINTS:

Would you rather
grow a horsetail
or
have scaly skin like a fish?

WINNER: POINTS:

Would you rather

be the host of your own talk show

or

the star of a Broadway show?

WINNER: POINTS:

Would you rather

find out that your best friend is an alien from another planet

or

a werewolf?

WINNER: POINTS:

Would you rather
ride on the back of a killer whale
or
a saber-toothed tiger?

WINNER: POINTS:

Would you rather
win a lifetime supply of clothes from one store
or
$500 to spend in any store you wanted?

WINNER: POINTS:

Would you rather
be an Olympic bobsledder
or
a sword-swallower?

WINNER: POINTS:

Would you rather
find a fingernail in your soup
or
a used Band-Aid in your mashed potatoes?

WINNER: POINTS:

Would you rather

have an inflatable bouncy house in your bedroom

or

a slide that leads to the outside?

WINNER: POINTS:

Would you rather

be stuck in the middle of the ocean in a rowboat

or

in the desert on a skateboard?

WINNER: POINTS:

Would you rather
sleep with a blanket made
out of sandpaper
or
tree bark?

WINNER: POINTS:

Would you rather
have a seashell for a nose
or
a pine cone?

WINNER: POINTS:

Would you rather

give an alligator a bath

or

swim in a pool with a shark?

WINNER: POINTS:

Would you rather

eat tuna fish–flavored ice cream

or

drink a garlic-flavored milkshake?

WINNER: POINTS:

Would you rather
hop from place to place
like a frog
or
slither around
like a snake?

WINNER: POINTS:

Would you rather
walk a mile on a slippery sheet of ice
or
through thick mud?

WINNER: POINTS:

TIEBREAKER

Would you rather

have a photographic memory

or

psychic abilities?

WINNER: POINTS:

WINNER: ______________________

TOTAL POINTS: ______________________

LEVEL 3

Savvy Selections

Would you rather

carry a 10-pound bowling ball with you everywhere you went for a week

or

a large cactus?

WINNER: POINTS:

Would you rather

spend a day completely submerged in butter

or

covered in superglue?

WINNER: POINTS:

Would you rather
have a multilevel tree house
with electricity in your backyard
or
an in-ground pool
with a waterslide?

WINNER: POINTS:

Would you rather
have four legs
or
a second pair of eyes
in the back of your head?

WINNER: POINTS:

Would you rather
eat birthday cake
with brussels sprout filling
or
mustard-flavored icing?

WINNER: POINTS:

Would you rather
receive a brand-new car on
the day you get your driver's license
or
a check for $10,000?

WINNER: POINTS:

Would you rather
work as a stunt person
or
as a bodyguard for a celebrity?

WINNER: POINTS:

Would you rather
have movie star parents
or
a sibling who's a
professional athlete?

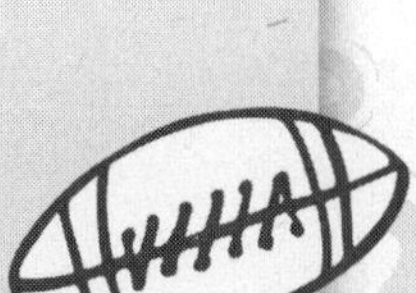

WINNER: POINTS:

Would you rather

wake up in a parallel universe
where talking dogs are
in charge of the planet

or

where robots are the
world's leaders?

WINNER: POINTS:

Would you rather

spend a day wearing wet jeans

or

shoes that are two sizes too small?

WINNER: POINTS:

Would you rather
brush your teeth with
pickle-flavored toothpaste
or
wash your body with
onion-scented soap?

WINNER: POINTS:

Would you rather
win a lifetime supply of
your favorite candy
or
movie tickets?

WINNER: POINTS:

Would you rather

live in a house with 30 pet cats

or

15 pet guinea pigs?

WINNER: POINTS:

Would you rather

walk around the mall in a full suit of armor

or

a gymnastics leotard?

WINNER: POINTS:

Would you rather

have your face added to Mount Rushmore

or

receive a star on the Hollywood Walk of Fame?

WINNER: POINTS:

Would you rather

chew on a piece of tinfoil

or

have sand stuck in your teeth?

WINNER: POINTS:

Would you rather
have your laugh replaced
by the sound of an air horn
or
a wailing siren?

WINNER: POINTS:

Would you rather
fall on a fragile school project
you just spent two hours making
or
drop a birthday cake you baked for
a family member in the dirt?

WINNER: POINTS:

Would you rather

drink a gallon of milk minutes before sprinting in a track meet

or

eat an entire pizza just before riding a roller coaster?

WINNER: POINTS:

Would you rather

interview a soldier from the American Revolutionary War

or

a knight from the Middle Ages?

WINNER: POINTS:

TIEBREAKER

Would you rather

be stuck at the top
of a Ferris wheel

or

in a graveyard at night?

WINNER: POINTS:

WINNER: ______________________________

TOTAL POINTS: ______________________________

LEVEL

4

Challenging Choices

Would you rather
spend a night trapped
in an amusement park
or
a zoo?

WINNER: POINTS:

Would you rather
be the size of an ant
for an entire week
or
the size of a giraffe?

WINNER: POINTS:

Would you rather

be face-to-face with Dracula

or

the Loch Ness Monster?

WINNER: POINTS:

Would you rather

find a backpack full of diamonds

or

an old trunk filled with gold?

WINNER: POINTS:

Would you rather
fly in a hot-air balloon over the countryside
or
ride in a helicopter over a famous city?

WINNER: POINTS:

Would you rather
drive the world's fastest car
or
be a passenger on the world's fastest airplane?

WINNER: POINTS:

Would you rather
get sprayed with a hose
on a freezing cold day
or
sit in a hot tub on a
sizzling summer day?

WINNER: POINTS:

Would you rather
eat a bagel
covered in earwax
or
boogers?

WINNER: POINTS:

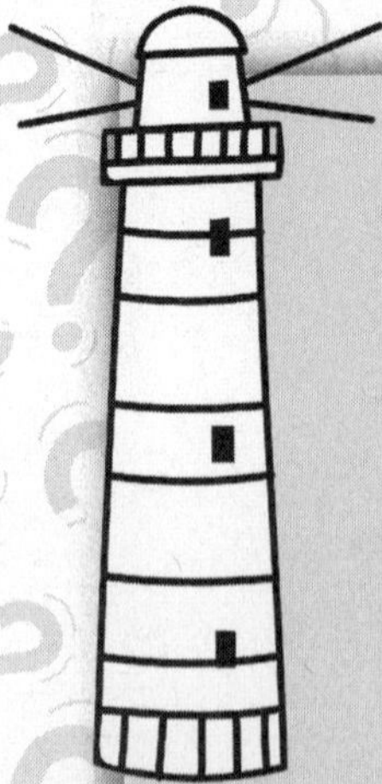

Would you rather
work as a lighthouse
keeper
or
a railroad
conductor?

WINNER: POINTS:

Would you rather
study pandas in their
natural habitat
or
observe the migration patterns
of penguins?

WINNER: POINTS:

Would you rather
be the world's best chess master
or
Ping-Pong player?

WINNER: POINTS:

Would you rather
eat a jar of mayonnaise
or
drink a bottle of cooking oil?

WINNER: POINTS:

Would you rather
be able to shoot lightning
out of your fingertips
or
create hurricane-force
winds with your mind?

WINNER: POINTS:

Would you rather
eat a live snail
or
a dead bumblebee?

WINNER: POINTS:

Would you rather

have peacock feathers

or

tiger-striped skin?

WINNER: POINTS:

Would you rather

have to rescue a hostage from an underground dungeon protected by guards

or

from a pirate ship?

WINNER: POINTS:

Would you rather
live on a cruise ship that
always travels to new destinations
or
in a beachfront mansion?

WINNER: POINTS:

Would you rather
work as an
undercover CIA agent
or
as a nuclear
engineer?

WINNER: POINTS:

Would you rather

take a ride on a magic carpet

or

on a flying broomstick?

WINNER: POINTS:

Would you rather

sprain your ankle the day before a championship basketball game

or

lose your voice the night of the school musical?

WINNER: POINTS:

TIEBREAKER

Would you rather

hike to the top of a volcano

or

take a tour of an old gold mine?

WINNER: POINTS:

WINNER: ______________________________

TOTAL POINTS: ______________________________

LEVEL 5

Difficult Decisions

Would you rather

accidentally kill your friend's plants that they've been growing for years

or

their pet goldfish?

WINNER: POINTS:

Would you rather

go paintballing with your school principal

or

play laser tag against all of your teachers?

WINNER: POINTS:

Would you rather
salsa dance with a ninja
or
a zombie?

WINNER: POINTS:

Would you rather
be a character in a movie
or
in a book?

WINNER: POINTS:

Would you rather
give up eating in restaurants
for the rest of your life
or
going to see movies
in movie theaters?

WINNER: POINTS:

Would you rather
win an award in school
for being the kindest student
or
the smartest?

WINNER: POINTS:

Would you rather

win a trip to an amusement park but get the flu the day you arrive

or

win a trip to a tropical island where it rains every day?

WINNER: POINTS:

Would you rather

take a bath in a tub full of macaroni and cheese

or

a shower under a stream of barbecue sauce?

WINNER: POINTS:

Would you rather

run 10 miles with an ingrown toenail

or

walk barefoot for 20 miles
on gravel roads?

WINNER: POINTS:

Would you rather

sing in front of
10 of your classmates

or

perform a choreographed
dance routine in front of
50 strangers?

WINNER: POINTS:

Would you rather
ride down the world's tallest waterslide
or
jump on the world's largest trampoline?

WINNER: POINTS:

Would you rather
meet your favorite celebrity and find out they're mean
or
never have a chance to meet them at all?

WINNER: POINTS:

Would you rather
play a game of soccer
while wearing flip-flops
or
a game of baseball using
an oven mitt instead
of a baseball glove?

WINNER: POINTS:

Would you rather
be the shortest
person in the world
or
the tallest?

WINNER: POINTS:

Would you rather
have a tutor who does
your homework
or
a personal chef who prepares
any food you want?

WINNER: POINTS:

Would you rather
live in the apartment below
professional yodelers
or
the drummer for
a heavy metal band?

WINNER: POINTS:

Would you rather
become best friends with the son or daughter of a famous celebrity
or
be the child of the president of the United States?

WINNER: POINTS:

Would you rather
spend a week trapped inside the body of a dolphin that lives in an aquarium
or
a tropical fish that lives in its natural habitat?

WINNER: POINTS:

Would you rather

have a glob of grape jelly fly out of your throat every time you cough

or

ketchup come out of your nose whenever you sneeze?

WINNER: POINTS:

Would you rather

be able to understand any language

or

know how to play any instrument?

WINNER: POINTS:

TIEBREAKER

Would you rather

have your personal diary read aloud to the whole school once

or

have an embarrassing video of you posted on YouTube for a year?

WINNER: POINTS:

WINNER: ____________________

TOTAL POINTS: ____________________

LEVEL 6

Clever Contests

Would you rather
spend the day living
inside the setting
of your favorite book
or
your favorite video game?

WINNER: POINTS:

Would you rather
go outside to find it
raining hot sauce
or
ranch dressing?

WINNER: POINTS:

Would you rather

be the leader of an
underwater world filled with
talking sea creatures

or

a jungle kingdom inhabited
by talking animals?

WINNER: POINTS:

Would you rather

get every question wrong
on a game show

or

forget all the words to
your song on a singing show?

WINNER: POINTS:

Would you rather

have music come on every time you walked into a room

or

an automatic laugh track play every time you made a joke?

WINNER: POINTS:

Would you rather

have a nightmare once a week

or

a fairly bad dream every night of the week?

WINNER: POINTS:

Would you rather

eat a cake that was made using salt instead of sugar

or

a batch of cookies made with chunks of fish in place of chocolate chips?

WINNER: POINTS:

Would you rather

open your backpack to find a rotten banana

or

expired bologna?

WINNER: POINTS:

Would you rather

live a double life as a superhero who secretly saves hundreds of people

or

save one person and be praised as a local hero?

WINNER: POINTS:

Would you rather

travel back in time to find out what really happened to Amelia Earhart

or

discover the truth about how Stonehenge was built?

WINNER: POINTS:

Would you rather

share a sleeping bag
with a nonvenomous snake

or

sleep in a small room
with an angry wasp?

WINNER: POINTS:

Would you rather

get stuck in an elevator
for 24 hours with a smelly person

or

be stuck in a dark cave
for 24 hours by yourself?

WINNER: POINTS:

Would you rather
time travel to a day 100 years ago
or
a day 100 years in the future?

WINNER: POINTS:

Would you rather
live in a house made
entirely out of cheese
or
crackers?

WINNER: POINTS:

Would you rather
have a national holiday
created in your honor
or
a large monument built for you?

WINNER: POINTS:

Would you rather
live on the top floor
of a skyscraper in a big city
or
in a beachfront hut on an island?

WINNER: POINTS:

Would you rather

be forced to wear a fake witch nose on school picture day

or

a clown wig?

WINNER: POINTS:

Would you rather

be celebrated for an achievement that wasn't yours

or

watch another person take credit for something you accomplished?

WINNER: POINTS:

Would you rather
go to a school that holds
all of its classes outside
or
takes its students on a field trip
once every month?

WINNER: POINTS:

Would you rather
get locked in a porta-potty overnight
or
a school locker?

WINNER: POINTS:

TIEBREAKER

Would you rather

eat a fried toad

or

a fried raccoon?

WINNER: POINTS:

WINNER: ______________________________

TOTAL POINTS: ______________________________

LEVEL

7

Brainy Battles

Would you rather
have a self-driving car
or
a car that can fly?

WINNER: POINTS:

Would you rather
bike two
miles uphill
or
swim one mile against
the current?

WINNER: POINTS:

Would you rather

your bedroom smell like
the inside of a sweaty
gym sneaker

or

raw sewage?

WINNER: POINTS:

Would you rather

be able to walk on water

or

through fire?

WINNER: POINTS:

Would you rather
complete an obstacle course
in high heels
or
a swimming race
in a puffy winter coat?

WINNER: POINTS:

Would you rather
put your retainer back
in your mouth after it fell into
the cafeteria garbage can
or
eat a sandwich out of a dumpster?

WINNER: POINTS:

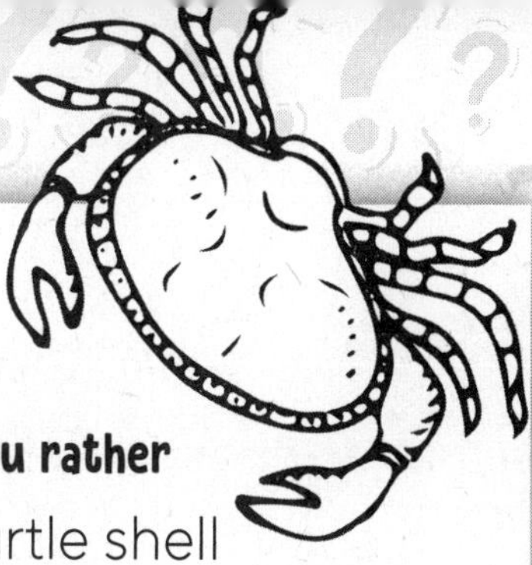

Would you rather

have a turtle shell

or

crab claws?

WINNER: POINTS:

Would you rather

referee the Super Bowl

or

be a judge at the Olympic Games?

WINNER: POINTS:

Would you rather

have access to a library that contains a copy of every book ever written

or

a museum that houses every dinosaur bone that's ever been discovered?

WINNER: POINTS:

Would you rather

have a neighbor who cuts down trees with a chain saw every night at 11:00 p.m.

or

shoots off fireworks every morning at 6:00 a.m.?

WINNER: POINTS:

Would you rather

eat your dog's vomit
every day for a week

or

swallow a live spider
every day for a month?

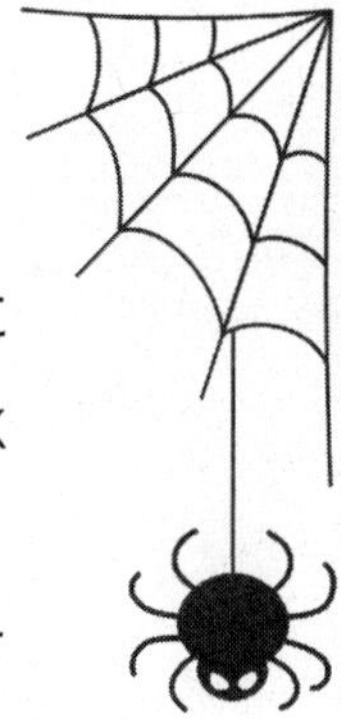

WINNER: POINTS:

Would you rather

have a $10 bill that regenerates
every time you spend it

or

an unlimited amount of pennies?

WINNER: POINTS:

Would you rather

have hands in place of your feet

or

feet in place of your hands?

WINNER: POINTS:

Would you rather

lose the money that was going
to pay for a big school field trip

or

lose clothing donations that your
classmates collected for kids in need?

WINNER: POINTS:

Would you rather

bungee jump off a tall building
in a bustling city

or

off a bridge over a large river?

WINNER: POINTS:

Would you rather

trade lives for a day
with a professional wrestler

or

a news reporter?

WINNER: POINTS:

Would you rather
have your favorite author
answer all of your questions
or
read a copy of the sequel
to your favorite book
before anyone else?

WINNER: POINTS:

Would you rather
get sprayed by a
skunk moments before
attending an
important event
or
peed on by a horse?

WINNER: POINTS:

Would you rather

lead an organization that brings an end to animal cruelty

or

that reverses the effects of air pollution?

WINNER: POINTS:

Would you rather

grow a giant horn from the center of your forehead

or

a pair of tiny, nonfunctional wings?

WINNER: POINTS:

TIEBREAKER

Would you rather

get caught in a powerful rainstorm without an umbrella

or

in a blizzard without a coat?

WINNER: POINTS:

WINNER

WINNER: ______________________________

TOTAL POINTS: ______________________________

LEVEL 8

Master's Match

Would you rather

spend the night alone
in your house after
watching a horror film

or

in a haunted house with
one other person?

WINNER: POINTS:

Would you rather

constantly have dry, itchy skin

or

clammy, sweaty hands?

WINNER: POINTS:

Would you rather

have everything you eat
taste like rotten eggs

or

everything you drink
taste like spoiled milk?

WINNER: POINTS:

Would you rather

go a year without
taking a shower

or

6 months without brushing
your teeth?

WINNER: POINTS:

Would you rather
find a stranger's hair in your meal after you've eaten most of it
or
a dead insect in the dessert you almost finished?

WINNER: POINTS:

Would you rather
have the ability to communicate with animals
or
choose 10 people's minds to read anytime you want?

WINNER: POINTS:

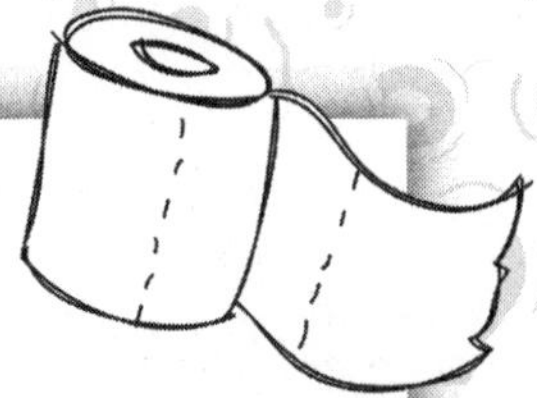

Would you rather

lick a toilet bowl in a public restroom

or

a handrail at Disney World?

WINNER: POINTS:

Would you rather

pop a stranger's pimple

or

rub cream on their rash?

WINNER: POINTS:

Would you rather

play the lottery and win
one lump sum of $500,000

or

win $1,000 a week for
the next 20 years?

WINNER: POINTS:

Would you rather

wake up at a sleepover
to discover your friends cut your
hair into a Mohawk

or

shaved off both of your eyebrows?

WINNER: POINTS:

Would you rather
drink a cow's milk
directly from its udders
or
take a bite of
honey straight from
a beehive?

WINNER: POINTS:

Would you rather
hear a loud ringing sound in your
ears for the rest of your life
or
have an itch that never goes away
even when you scratch it?

WINNER: POINTS:

Would you rather

be able to communicate with the dead

or

with other people telepathically?

WINNER: POINTS:

Would you rather

lick a dusty bookshelf

or

take a bite out of a chunk of mold?

WINNER: POINTS:

Would you rather
have the ability to teleport
or
to fly?

WINNER: POINTS:

Would you rather
know all of history
or
have the ability to
predict the future?

WINNER: POINTS:

Would you rather
lick a slimy slug
or
have a camel lick the inside of your mouth?

WINNER: POINTS:

Would you rather
let your fingernails grow 11 inches long
or
go 6 months without washing your feet?

WINNER: POINTS:

Would you rather
drink a magical potion
that gives you
superhuman strength
or
speed?

WINNER: POINTS:

Would you rather
eat a doughnut with
insect guts as frosting
or
a slice of pizza topped
with snakeskin?

WINNER: POINTS:

TIEBREAKER

Would you rather

be an expert archer

or

a professional fencer?

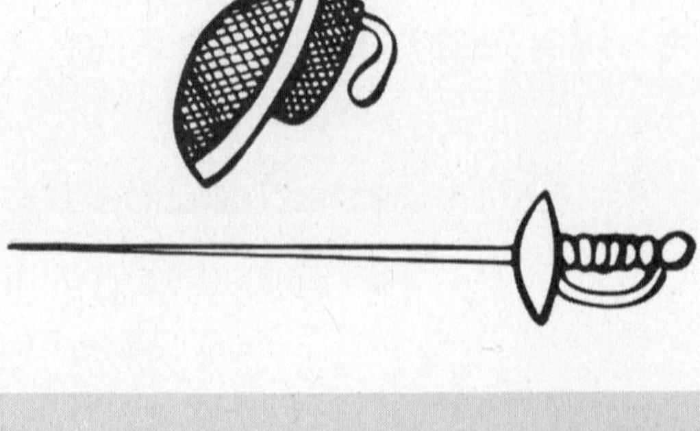

WINNER: POINTS:

WINNER: ______________________________

TOTAL POINTS: ______________________________

WINNER
Would You Rather?
MADE YOU THINK! EDITION

This certificate
is awarded to

____

for being a legend of logic,
a heavyweight of humor,
and a captain of creativity!

Tough choices are
no match for you.

CONGRATULATIONS!

About the Author

Lindsey Daly grew up in Andover, New Jersey. She graduated from Ramapo College of New Jersey with a BA in History and a certification in Secondary Education. Lindsey is a middle school social studies teacher and the author of the bestselling Would You Rather? series. She lives with her dog, Teddy, in New Jersey.

Parents, for more information about Lindsey and her books, follow her online:

Instagram: **@lindseydalybooks**

Twitter: **@LindseyDaly10**